GOD IS ENERGY. DO YOU BELIEVE?

Using Science and Creation to explain our existence.

SEMISI PONE
BSc, MSc (Hons). Auckland.

Copyright © Rainbow Enterprises 2014

Publisher: Rainbow Enterprises 2014

ISBN: 978-0-9941075-4-1

All rights reserved. No part of this publication maybe reproduced or transmitted in any form or by any means, electronic or mechanical, including photocopy, recording or any information storage or retrieval system, without permission in writing from the copyright holder or publisher.

Rainbow Enterprises is the trade/publisher name of Semisi Pule aka Semisi Pule Pone.

Email: semisipone@yahoo.com
       jaybod100@hotmail.com
       rainbowenterprises7@gmail.com

Revised 3rd Edition. March 2014.

Acknowledgement.

This book includes some notes taken from the King James Bible and the Penguin encyclopedia.

EDUCATION

My brain was empty
Then I learned the ABC
My mind was blind
Then I learned designs
Now I can see
As far as Eternity…

From "Rhymes of an Aspiring Writer" by Semisi Pone.

Introduction.

I want to write this book from my own perspective and experience. I am sure you do not want too many complicated scientific explanations and theories. I am putting forward my idea like a conversation with your neighbour. It will be easy to understand.

I will use the bible and some "universal truths" to explain what I believe is the ultimate destiny of man. Our existence cannot be purposeless as evolution proposes. Just a mistake in the scheme of things on our planet and the universe.

Universal truths are scientific theories which have a lot of evidence supporting it and accepted by everyone.

We are all fascinated by our own mortality, the origin of mankind, the universe, God, creation and what happens when we die. Most people go to Church and involve themselves in religious activities as preparation for their "after life". Saving themselves from the eternal fires of hell. Perhaps the red giant that the sun will become before its final demise.

Maybe the expansion of the sun is the hell the bible is talking about. In that case, no one will escape. The whole earth will be burned to ashes. The sun will grow into a red giant and collapse into a "white dwarf" or "black hole". Of course, it will take a long time, millions of years perhaps. Nothing is quick in the universe, in man years.

Only energy will escape to space. It cannot be destroyed according to scientific laws.

"Energy cannot be created or destroyed. It can only be transformed from one form into another".

For example, it can be transferred from solar energy into heat energy or mechanical energy and so on. They are manifestations of energy. It is an abstract, calculable quantity associated with the physical processes.

I am hoping to make a good argument that man will escape the burning earth as an "Energy Being", indestructible energy, as proposed by scientists, and populate planets in other solar systems or maybe galaxies far, far away.

We cannot travel by spaceship they are too slow and perishable. The quickest spaceship on earth can only travel at about 20,000 km/hr.

Man can travel as an Energy Being at the speed of light or faster. Light travels through space at 300,000 km/second.

However, Einstein did propose that nothing can travel faster than light. If it does, time will go backwards, in his "Twin Paradox".

Man as an "Energy or Super Being" will exist like God. It is indestructible and last forever. There will be no beginning or end. Time and space will become irrelevant.

When you live forever, travelling to other solar systems, stars or galaxies is not a problem. You travel at 300,000 km/second, you have all the time in the universe to get there. 1 billion years will be just a moment. 1 billion kilometres will be just a "hop down the road".

It will be interesting if we can recover our "galactic" memory, perhaps we may find out where we have been before we populated earth. The planets where we have lived, the solar systems we populated, the galaxies we visited in our existence before earth. It will be the greatest story of all time.

Enjoy.

CONTENTS.

CHAPTER 1.   CREATION...................9

CHAPTER 2.   EVOLUTION................15

CHAPTER 3.   GOD...........................19

CHAPTER 4.   ENERGY...................26

CHAPTER 5.   THE ENERGY BEING...31

CHAPTER 6.   CONCLUSIONS...........41

CHAPTER 1. CREATION.

God said, "Let there be light". And it was done. God said, "Let there be a heaven and earth, land and seas and plants and animals". And it was done. God created everything that he thought was necessary for earth.

Then God saw his creation was not complete. Everything was there except somebody to rule over the earth. So he created man in his image, from the dust of the earth. The very first human being, Adam.

Adam lived happily in the Garden of Eden with all the animals and the plants but he was not happy. God saw Adam's unhappiness and he thought that perhaps he needs a companion. So he took a bone from his rib cage and created the first woman, Eve.

Adam and Eve lived happily in the Garden of Eden, with everything provided for them by God. But there was one tree that God forbid them to touch, the tree of "good and evil". God said unto them, "You can have everything that is in the Garden of Eden, but do not eat from the tree of "good and evil", for the day you eat from it; you shall surely die".

Then one day the serpent saw how happy Adam and Eve were, he was jealous of Gods creation. So he decided to ruin their lives forever. He said to Eve, "Is it true that God forbid you from eating from that tree?". Eve replied, "Yes. God told us we will die if we eat from that tree".

"God is not telling you the truth. He knows when you eat from that tree, you will become like him. You will become Gods, knowing good and evil", the devil said through the snake.

One day Eve saw how juicy the fruit looked and how inviting it is, she decided to try it. Maybe the serpent was right. She took a fruit from it and bit into it. Then she gave it to Adam who also bit from the fruit.

Then God opened their eyes and they realise they are naked. They were ashamed. They ran and hid in the bushes. God called them. "Adam, Eve", did I not tell you not to eat from that tree? Did I not tell you that you will die if you eat from it? From now on you will have to sweat for your food and drink. From now on you shall bear children in pain and die and return to the dust of the earth. You are banished forever from the Garden of Eden".

God also punished the serpent. "You shall crawl on your stomach and eat dust forever", God said to the serpent.

Adam and Eve ran away and lived as nomads, wandering the desert and feeding off its meagre offerings. They learned to domesticate animals and plants. They also bore 2 children, Cain and Abel.

One day Cain and Abel went to their garden, each with offerings to God.

Abel chose the best animal from his farm for his offering. Cain chose the worst from his crops for his offering. God saw Cain's heart was not good and he did not accept his sacrifice. He accepted Abel's who had a good heart. Cain was outraged that God accepted his brothers offering instead of his, so he killed him.

God said to Cain, "You have murdered your brother in your jealousy. You are banished to wander the earth. You shall not return to your parents". "But God, I might be killed by others if they find me", Cain protested. "No I will mark your forehead, no one will touch you", God said.

Cain wandered the earth. The bible say that he met other people and had children. **It is a question as to where those people came from.**
Perhaps God created more people when he was disappointed with Adam and Eve? The bible does not say where they came from. Maybe God also created others.

Adam and Eve had a third child named Seth and younger children as well.

The story of creation is probably the most read and most debated of all time. All Christians around the world study it and try to explain the scriptures. I think it is straight forward. God created everything. That's it. That is creation. God spoke and it was done.

There are 39 books in the Bible's Old Testament. All of them put a little light on creation and how God interacts with man.

The most common pattern is that God is revered by man. God will punish those who are sinful. The laws of Moses or the 10 Commandments was the ultimate judge of all men, at least in the known world of that time.

The Bible's New Testament approaches the rules of engagement differently. In the books of Matthew, Mark, Luke and John, they tell of the birth and life of Jesus Christ. He was the son of God. He came to fulfil the prophesies of the Old Testament and to save mankind from their sins, probably the fault of Eve and Adam by eating the fruit of "good and evil".

Jesus said, "I am the way, the truth and the life. No one can come to the father but by me". Christians believe in heaven and hell. Heaven is where the father is or God, good people go to heaven. It is like paradise.

Hell is where the bad people are sent. They burn in its eternal fires forever, gnashing their teeth and crying out for some water to cool their sinful tongues.

The whole of the New Testament revolve around the life and teachings of Jesus Christ and his 12 disciples.

In John 3:16, Jesus promised heaven to all the believers, **"For God so loved the world that he gave his only begotten son, that whoever believes in him; shall not perish but have everlasting life".**

The essence of the Christian faith is acceptance of Jesus Christ as their saviour by asking him to live their lives through him. That is the faith that will ultimately take them to heaven and everlasting life.

In the 10 commandments, God imposes the "tooth for a tooth" law. It was very tough on the followers of Moses. Moses proposed killing your enemy.

However, Jesus changed it into "turning the other cheek" which was also very tough for his followers. If your enemy slaps you in the face, give them the other cheek to slap as well. It was "submission" in a sense.

The 27 books of the new Testament follows the same teachings and extrapolate on the teachings of Christ.

It appears that Creation as we know it only ended in death, Adam and Eve's punishment. Christ came to give man everlasting life. To save man from the punishment given to Adam and Eve.

A lot of people do not believe there is life after death. It seems that everything ends **"when dust returns to dust"**. So what is the purpose of being born, live for a few years, maybe 100, then die forever? The universe is billions of years old. To only live in 100 years out of those billions of years is like a spark in the scheme of things in the Universe. A spark is maybe too long, but there is nothing else to describe how insignificant that existence is. How purposeless and meaningless it is.

Christ proposed that we will live forever as Spirit Beings, as part of the Holy Ghost, the Third Trinity.

When you die, your earthly body decomposes and return to the dust. Your spirit returns to the Holy Ghost, to God, where it came from in the first place. Man's immortal soul.

In the fourth chapter on "Energy" I will try to link the Spiritual Being and the Energy Being to **"prove"** that it is one and the same thing. Perhaps the ancients knew more than they wrote down?
Creation and Christianity is very straight forward. All you have to do as a Christian is believe in Jesus Christ as your saviour and he will do the rest through the Holy Spirit.
It seems that Adam and Eve's original sin, of disobeying God, necessitates the action of Christ, to bring man back to God.

The three Trinity. God the father, God the Son and the Holy Ghost are the three manifestations of God. Man will ultimately live forever as part of the Holy Ghost. As a "Spirit Being". It is the crown jewel of Gods creation. That is what the bible means by "everlasting life".

You cannot live forever as a human being. The flesh will die and decompose, it is your spirit that will live forever according to the bible. That is the whole Christian faith in a sentence.

Christ came to earth to save that spirit from God's original punishment of Adam and Eve and bring it back to him.

CHAPTER 2. EVOLUTION.

Scientists believe that mankind developed, through millions of years, from inanimate compounds. In the beginning when there was nothing but the "primordial soup" on the surface of the earth, lighting strikes the compounds and fused them to become a "cell". It behaved like a single celled animal and started to divide. Perhaps over millions of years, and through natural selection, a single celled animal arose from those inanimate compounds.

The cell evolved into simple animals and plants and gradually developed into more complex organisms through "selection".

Natural selection was proposed by British Scientist, Charles Darwin. In his day it was ridiculed, that man's ancestor was a monkey. Natural selection is the process where organisms which adapt or are suited for the environment survive while the others die off. For example, if the cells can survive in the methane atmosphere of the original primordial soup, they will live. Those that cannot survive in the methane atmosphere will die. Survival of the fittest.

A more straightforward example would be, "If bald men are not accepted by women then they will not marry and the "baldness gene" will die off, because it's not wanted. The selection pressure is against baldness. The gene for baldness will die. It will not be passed on to later generations".

Another example is, "If all ugly women are not accepted by men. Their gene will die off because they will not reproduce and the gene for being ugly is not passed on".

To explain how this works, every man and woman have genes in their chromosomes that contains the information which dictate everything in their development. Almost like a computer programme controlling the internet for example.

When the sperm is passed to the woman, it fuses with the egg in her womb, then develop into a foetus. The foetus contains the same information from the mother (egg) and the father (sperm). It will develop according to the information received from its parents.

The way it looks, how tall he/she is, what coloured skin, hair, bald or not and so on.

Half of the genes are from the donor of the sperm or father. Half of the genes are from the mother. If the father is not bald or does not have genes for baldness. None of his children or grandchildren will be bald. The gene for "baldness" is selected against and will die out or become "extinct". Sometimes the females or mothers carry the gene from their ancestors, but through "selection pressure" over generations it will be slowly "weeded out" by nature. That is what Natural Selection is.

The same process applies to any other gene, like ugliness, disability, intelligence, stupidity and so on.

Sometimes, it is the environment that ultimately affects the expression of a gene. For example, if an intelligent baby is born into a stupid society, he or she "learns" to be stupid until she moves to an "intelligent" society where her intelligence is expressed by learning from intelligent people around him or her. A bit humorous but it explains the point.

Another example is skin colour. Sometimes brown parents have white children. It is because they carry the gene from their ancestors. They probably have white ancestors or Europeans who gave them the gene for white skin and a lot of other traits that may be "hidden" and expressed generations down the line.

The theory of evolution has become a lot more complicated since Charles Darwin. Scientists now study natural selection at the molecular level. At the chromosome and genetic level which ultimately explains why things are the way they are with living organisms.

In Darwin's day, it was the physical characteristics like different beak sizes in finches or the variety of shapes of flowers and so on. Now Scientists are studying why and how genes work. How does nature store that information inside the genes? And pass it on for millions of years? Computer programmes will not last that long.

Computer programmes are not as complicated or as vast as genetic information. A single gene contains information that can be stored in a lot of computers, maybe thousands or millions. Yet you cannot see a gene, it is very, very, very small.

In summary, in the beginning when there was nothing on earth; just the primordial soup and a methane atmosphere, lighting hit some inanimate compounds and fused them to become the "first living organism". They behaved like living organisms and divided like a living cell.

Eventually over time and through natural selection, it developed into single then multi-celled organisms. Then it developed into complex organisms, then fish, then developed legs and lungs and invaded land. Then it developed into different types of animals, became a monkey then man. Similarly, other organisms, for example, fishes and plants evolved in the same way. It probably took billions of years. That is the theory of Evolution in 2 paragraphs.

CHAPTER 3. GOD.

The concept of God is a very complex and difficult one to explain, even by Ministers of the Christian Churches. When I was young and used to attend Church every Sunday, we were told that God came from God. It was sufficient explanation in those days. As I grew older and went to school then University, I learned other theories like Evolution, for example. God became even bigger and more complex as I learned more.

Then I learned about the Universe and how vast it is, I became even more intrigued. Now God is so big, it's as large as the Universe itself, or bigger.

To give you an idea of how large the Universe is, consider the nearest star to our sun or solar system. It is called by Scientists "Proxima Centauri". It is 4 light years away, from earth. A light year is the distance that light travels, through space, in one year.

Light travels at 300,000 km per second. In 1 year it will travel 9,500,000,000,000 kilometres. In 4 years, it would have travelled 38 billion kilometres. It is a huge number. Our fastest spaceship will take a long, long, long, long time to get there, 190,000 years at 20,000 kilometres per hour! There is no way we can travel anywhere in our spaceships.

Some stars are up to a thousand light years away from us! And that is just in our galaxy, the Milky Way. There are other galaxies, billions of galaxies, in the universe and they maybe billions of light years away! It is mind boggling how vast the Universe is. Scientists even have the pictures of those galaxies in your Science Text books at school.

If God created all of that, it is unimaginable how powerful God is. It is a bit difficult to think that everything including the creation of the Universe was just a mistake. Natural selection having the final word.

I propose that God is Energy. The whole earth is held together and made up of energy. The whole Universe is made up of energy. God is Energy. What holds the sun, solar system and galaxies in place? In the emptiness of space? They are not just floating !

Our sun gives energy to plants which use it to make carbohydrates and protein which sustain all other living organisms on Earth. Scientists say that this energy from the sun comes in electromagnetic waves. It is also proposed that within the electromagnetic waves there are particles.

So light is made up of particles that flow like a wave. In this case, an electromagnetic wave. Energy may be stored inside those particles. Just a description of this kind of energy. Just like all other forms of energy, thermal, mechanical, heat, nuclear and so on. All manifestations of the same thing. No one can explain what it is yet.

The Penguin Encyclopedia describes energy as ***"an abstract calculable quantity associated with all physical processes and objects whose total value is conserved"***.

A bit vague. I think what they mean is that the total value of the energy is never lost.

In other words, "energy cannot be created or destroyed, only transformed from one form into another". For example, from thermal into mechanical then heat. Like steam powering a paddle boat on the Mississippi river. The steam turns the engine which turns the paddle. That is thermal energy, steam, converted into mechanical energy, the paddle moving. There is also heat generated by the friction between the paddle and the water, heat energy.

God is an enigma. No one really knows where God came from or how he operates. Or how he created the Universe. Scientists have a lot of theories about how the Universe started and how it continues to evolve and expand.

The Big Bang Theory is probably the most accepted.

However, according to the bible, in the beginning there was God and nothing else. The "word" was God. The word created everything. The word of God. So science and religion share this in common. They both agree that there was nothing in the beginning. Science believes that the "Big Bang" created the Universe. Religion believes that God created it. Religion believes that God has 3 manifestations or the 3 trinities. God the father. God the Son and God the Holy Ghost.

God the father created the heavens and the earth. God the son came to earth to save mankind from the punishment of Adam and Eve, and their sins.
When he returned to heaven he told his disciples he will sent them the "Holy Spirit" to guide them. It is the Holy Spirit that guide us today. The Holy Ghost.

When we die, we either return to God or burn in the eternal fires of hell. It is our spirit that God claims. As he said to Adam and Eve, their bodies will die and return to the dust from where it came.

It was Jesus who saved our spirit. God did not mention a spiritual being when he punished Adam and Eve from the Garden of Eden. The King James version of the bible does mention that God said "they", probably the 3 trinities, will not allow Adam to eat from the fruit of eternal life and live forever like God. God put an angel at the entrance to the Garden of Eden with a flaming sword to keep Adam and his descendants out of the Garden of Eden or they might eat from the fruit of eternal life and live forever.

So the idea of Eternal life came from God the Son, Jesus Christ. In John 3:16, it is said, ***"For God so loved the world that he gave his only begotten son; that whoever believes in him shall not perish but have everlasting life"***.

It appears that God the Son, Jesus Christ, gave his earthly body to die for our sins; the reasons why Adam and Eve were punished in the first place, so we can return to God. So we can have eternal life, which was taken away from Adam and Eve for disobeying God.

When God the Son, Jesus Christ, returned to heaven he promised his disciples he will send the Holy Ghost to be their helper.

All believers have to do is to invite God the Holy Ghost to live inside them and change their lives. Being "Born Again", as it is called by Christians around the world. We see it all the time on the Evangelical TV Programmes, believers praying to God the Holy Ghost to enter their bodies and become one with them.

To cleanse them of their sins so they become a new person, just like being born as a baby. It is this new person that Jesus Christ came to resurrect from the dust that Adam and Eve were punished to forever, by God the Father. God the Son, Jesus Christ, gave man a chance to live forever by sending God the Holy Ghost to save him, just like God the father's original intention with Adam and Eve.

It seems that we are all part of God. Our "immortal soul". The "Energy Being" or "Spirit".
Science explains how our bodies breakdown the food we eat into energy to sustain our bodies.

This energy then passes on into other forms of energy. It cannot be destroyed. When we die, our bodies decompose, but the energy that kept us going moves on to some other form. Is that our spirit? That energy that leaves our body when we die?

Does it go back to space, heaven or enter a new body as in reincarnation? Our bodies cannot live without that energy. It comes from the food as explained by scientists. That energy in the food came from the sun in particles riding the electromagnetic waves. Science explains that in the sun's core there is an "eternal nuclear furnace" breaking down the "nuclear" fuel and giving off a small percentage of that energy as electromagnetic waves which reaches earth, and the plants trap and convert it into carbohydrates and proteins to sustain all living organisms on earth. When those organisms die the energy moves on to other forms.

Is it God the Holy Ghost? Packaged in small amounts inside particles that are brought to earth by electromagnetic waves from the sun?

No one has been to the sun's core to see what is going on over there. All we have is the scientific theories to explain it. Is God inside the core of the sun? The bible says that God is "everywhere". Which means that God is part of everything. It is not limited to the sun only.

Maybe other galaxies, the whole universe as well. It is energy that drives the whole universe. That is one thing that is common to all parts of the Universe, Energy. So the bible may have explained God there. God is everything. God is energy, it is everywhere. It is part of everything. It holds everything in place.

God cannot exist without some kind of consciousness or intelligence. Science has yet to explain why we have the intelligence that we have. We all have the same brain cells but some people are smarter than others. Monkeys are not as smart as humans yet their brains are about the same size.

Maybe God the Holy Ghost provides that "consciousness". That "Energy" that seems to "go out of your eyes" when you die. That intelligence that is part of all living things. We have yet to measure the intelligence of inanimate beings or things.

We cannot because our current knowledge and technologies cannot explain it. Our human brains is not "smart" enough to work it out. Is the Universe as a collective part of God the Holy Ghost, intelligent? It must be. Otherwise, why do things happen as they do? It cannot be just a galactic mistake!

Is our whole existence and the universe a mistake? As proposed by some people? Natural Selection is not a mistake! There is a definite design there! All living things evolve to become better or more adapted to their environment. That is a definite design. Otherwise, animal evolution will be moving in different directions with no pattern whatsoever. Mistakes in nature are random they are not in a pattern.

The concept of God is becoming clearer, at least to me anyway.

CHAPTER 4. ENERGY.

Energy that gives us life comes from the sun. Scientists suggest that a small proportion of the energy generated in the sun's core travel to earth as light made up of electromagnetic waves. Particles of energy make up those electromagnetic waves. This energy is trapped by the chlorophyll in plants and used to make carbohydrates, proteins and other things that it needs. The carbohydrates and proteins sustain animals and fishes that feed on those plants including man.

This energy is passed on from the plants to primary feeders or herbivores then carnivores and so on in the food chain. Man is ultimately the top of the food chain. When we eat our food, whether they be plant or animal products our bodies digest the food and the energy is released to power our muscles, nerves, skeletal structure so that we can carry out our normal activities.

There are also other sources of energy like wind energy which is used to turn turbines and generate electricity. There is also wave energy, hydro-energy, fossil energy from coal, oil and so on. In fact there are a large number of energy sources. The sun's rays can also be trapped as solar energy. They are all different manifestations of the same thing.

As mentioned in the previous paragraph the Penguin Encyclopedia describe energy as **"an abstract calculable quantity associated with all physical processes and objects whose total value is conserved"**. This means the total value of the energy is never lost. It can only be transformed into another form. The whole world, both living and non-living are affected by energy in one form or another. Some energy from the sun may be lost into space or transformed into carbohydrates, or mechanical energy but the total will always be the same.

Sometime in the future, the sun will expand as it runs out of fuel in its core and earth will be burned to ashes. Energy will be transformed into another form, maybe heat and escape into space.
To explain this in more detail, according to scientists, when stars run out of fuel, they expand into a "red giant". Our sun which is 1.2 million kilometres in diameter will expand into 100 million kilometres in diameter or bigger.

The earth is 150 million kilometres from the sun. When the sun expands, it will be 100 million kilometres nearer to earth, its surface temperature will increase by a factor of 100,000s. In the core it is 15 million degrees centigrade. On the earth it may be more than 100,000 degrees centigrade on the surface. Not only from the sun being nearer, but also from the increased heat on its surface. That heat is probably enough to melt and turn the earth into ash, the other closer planets as well.

Mercury, Venus, Earth and Mars will turn into ash. The other planets Jupiter, Saturn, Uranus, Neptune and Pluto may be affected as well but they are a bit further away from the sun. Red Giants are often described as "cool", but that is probably in relation to other stars which may be hotter.

The sun will ultimately collapse after its initial expansion. If the speed of collapse is faster than the speed of light, 300,000 kilometres per second, it will turn into a "black hole" with nothing escaping out of it. Not even light. Otherwise it will turn into a "white dwarf" which is no bigger than earth, only about 12,000 kilometres across instead of 1.2 million kilometres across.

The planets that are still orbiting the sun will probably be flung into space as its gravitational pull is no longer enough to hold them in place. Forces on them might be enough to break them apart into asteroids or perhaps turn them into "wandering comets".

Attracted by the gravitational pull of distant stars or just evaporate.

The energy which has held our solar system together will probably "escape" into space or transformed into another form. The energy that was once part of us, keeping us alive, moving and operating will probably escape into space as well as heat, after the sun's heat burn our earthly bodies to ashes. Where does all the energy go?

Do they just form a wave and travel at the speed of light to be captured by distant stars, plants and so on? The energy that was once part of us is transformed into "waves of particles", wandering aimlessly in space until captured by the gravity of other solar systems and attracted to their living beings? It seems a bit chaotic and accidental.

The Universe is a very orderly place with everything in a pattern, proof of intelligent intervention. God's Creation?

Suppose God is energy, God is part of everything. Christians believe God is "everywhere". If God is energy, this belief will be true.

Energy is everywhere, it holds everything in the universe together. From huge galaxies millions of light years across to tiny atoms that we cannot even see with our most powerful electron microscope. This energy is so great that when released, like in an atomic bomb, it has colossal destructive power. The energy that holds the atom together.

Does energy have "consciousness"? Like a living being? It seems to be present everywhere, cannot be destroyed and transformed into one form or another. Scientists still cannot explain it.

Are "spirit beings" made of energy? There has been numerous reports of "ghosts" and "spirits" from all parts of the globe. Are they "Energy Beings" which have left their human form? The energy that was once driving the human body is now existing by itself as a "Spirit"?

Christians believe that when we die our spirits goes back to God. It may vary between different Churches and religions, but the principle is still the same.

When humans die their spirits go to God or heaven, paradise and so on. No one has bothered to explain "spirits" in scientific terms. Probably from the lack of evidence, but if billions of people believe it, for 2,000 or more years now; there must be something in it. It may be that in order to "see" the evidence scientist may have to look at this proposal from another angle. The spiritual angle.

If energy does have "consciousness", it may be possible for energy beings to exist, in whatever form as dictated by its environment. It will solve a lot of problems like time and space travel as energy beings are indestructible.

CHAPTER 5. THE ENERGY BEING

I have thought about the idea of man as a spirit for a long time, ever since I started going to Sunday school in our local Methodist Church as a child. Christians believe, and it is written in the bible, that there is life after death. When our earth bodies die and decompose, it returns to the earth…it becomes one with the earth. Dust return to dust as God said to Adam. But man's spirit lives on forever. It is this spirit that is a bit of an enigma, there is very little we know about man's spirit being. We know it lives inside us but that is about all. I would like to discuss the Spirit or Energy Being in more detail in this chapter.

There are several concepts or ideas that all refer to the Energy Being or the Spirit. In modern teachings of many "enlightened" people…it is referred to as the "inner self" or your inner voice or your gut feeling or instinct or mind or soul. We always refer to it as if it is somebody else. But no one has ever pointed out that all those concepts or ideas are all referring to the one and same thing. The Spirit or Energy Being inside all of us.

It is my view that the Spirit or Energy Being is the one who was made in the image of God. It is the all powerful person that performs miracles and is indestructible. Because it is energy it cannot be created or destroyed. It can take on many forms. It is intelligent and "all seeing". It knows everything and have power over everything. But how do we harness the power of that powerful indestructible being in us? How do we get it to do what we want?

When I was a salesman, one of the things that we were taught is called "affirmations". It is almost like meditation. Before entering somebody's house to make a presentation we were taught to perform an affirmation. It involves writing down the things you want to happen in that sales presentation and repeating it a hundred times or so to yourself before going into the house. You feel confident and focussed on what you want from that presentation. The customer will also feel the power and conviction of your presentation and will be more likely to buy your product. The same thing happens with missionaries when they preach to a group of non-believers. The listeners can feel the power of his convictions and faith and will want to join him and become a Christian. But who is the actual creator of that conversion? To make the sale? And to convert non-believers? Is it the Super Being inside us? The Energy Being? The Spirit? Are we just making the affirmations just like we are praying to him asking the Super Being to do things for us?

The power of prayer is well known amongst Christian believers. There are about 2-3 billion or more Christians on earth. They all believe in the power of prayer. When they pray they can feel the power of God, the presence of God amongst them. They feel peace. They feel blessed. They feel enlightened. They feel more powerful after prayer. Is it because they have awakened the Super Being inside them? The Spirit? When the Spirit or God takes over their lives and making decisions they do become like a super being themselves. They do things they normally would not do because they have faith in what they are doing. They believe that God will award them what they ask for. And it usually happens!

When I was a child going to Sunday school in our local Methodist Church in Tonga, I was brought up to believe that God can do anything.
That God can give you riches if you want. I believe it because I can see and feel it. The members of our church sometimes prepares a feast for the lay preacher or Minister and all the congregation are invited. There may be as many as 50-60 people coming to a feast. It happens very often especially on white Sundays, Christmas and New Year. Most of them did not have jobs. They get all the food for the feast from their gardens, livestock, fishing or donations from relatives. It did create a certain feeling in us children. We thought we were rich! We were eating like Kings very often! Our banquets included all the local delicacies, whole roast pigs and imported sweets. We feel that we have a life of abundance. We did not have any money. We have no need for it, but we had abundance of food and we loved it as kids. It was only when I went to University in New Zealand that I realise that the bigger countries think we are poor! That our income per capita is lower than most countries and we could not afford the trappings of a modern society like cars, television and overseas holidays. But do you really need those things? Do cars, televisions and holidays make you happy? We often hear about millionaires who are always depressed or suicidal despite their wealth.

When we consider the purpose of our existence. Why are we on earth? Was it an accident of nature? That lightning hit the primordial soup and fused inanimate compounds to become single celled animals? Which can reproduce and gave rise to all living things through evolution? An accident of nature? I don't think that the obvious design of nature is an accident. Accidents are random, they are not in a pattern like evolution. Evolution is a definite design.

Why is earth where it is and the stars and galaxies where they are? Why can't we travel to any of the stars, visit other solar systems and galaxies? Isn't it because man cannot build a spacecraft that is fast enough to get there in our lifetime? It will take something like 190,000 years to fly to the nearest star in our quickest spaceship. Man needs to think about this carefully. If he is not smart enough to build a spaceship to fly to the next star, then obviously he is not smart enough to interpret God's designs. I don't think it was the Big Bang that created the Universe, as some Scientists propose. But something similar with intelligent design. God put the solar systems around every star and stars in every galaxy. Man is just beginning to understand how things work in our bodies, on earth and in the universe. Is the Super or Energy Being in us God?

We know that sometimes certain people can perform miracles beyond our comprehension. It is impossible for the normal human being to do but it happens. Is it because those people are in touch with the Super Being or Energy Being inside them? They have learned to use its unlimited power? I think so. When we pray or perform affirmations or meditations we are trying to awaken the Energy Being in us to become one with us so we can use its super powers. Did Jesus know this?

When he told the disciples how to pray? He send them the Holy Spirit which came like a "tongue of fire" according to the bible. It allowed the disciples to perform miracles in the name of Jesus. The Roman Empire frowned upon the work of the early Christians and they were discriminated against. Tourists to-day can still visit the catacombs in Rome where the early Christians were buried. They were not allowed to bury their dead in Roman cemeteries so they dug up the earth and bury them underground. Needless to say the Christians great faith and the power of the Super or Energy Being within them won over the Roman Empire. The word of God dominated over the swords and spears of the Roman soldiers. Rome is now the centre of the largest of the Christian Churches. The Catholic Church.

Scientists can explain a lot of things about nature. We see miracles performed in the name of science everyday. The technology is so amazing to-day I can only say they are miracles. Modern medicine, radio, television, automobiles, telephones, computers, aircraft and so on. These are miracles performed by man. But where did man get his ideas? His inventions? His logic and inspiration? His enlightenment? Isn't it the Energy Being in all of us that is the creator? The all powerful, all knowing, all seeing Energy Being or Spirit in us? Isn't it the same being that brought down the Roman Empire in the name of Jesus Christ? The same being that came like a "tongue of fire" as the Holy Spirit? The same Super Being that guides your way every day and gives you everything that you need? If you take away that Super Being, what is left?

When we die our eyes look vacant and lifeless. It is opaque and unintelligible. Our bodies cannot move, then it starts to rot and decompose. Is it because the Energy Being that kept us alive has left our body? The Spirit has no more use for that body and left it? Then it becomes lifeless. The life giver is the Energy Being, Spirit or God? Just like a driver that turns off the ignition and left the car? The car, even though it is new, will start to rot or rust because there is no driver to turn it on and drive it?

Jesus has already taught us how to be in touch with the Super or Energy Being…through prayer. Some people also call it affirmations or meditation. If we need his help he is always there for us. The only time he is not with us is when we are dead. That means that he has left the earthly body. Some people believe that he takes on a new body like in reincarnation or he returns to God where he came from in the first place. Just like a little spaceship returning to the mother ship after its work is done.

So what is the point of it all? Are they aliens using the earth bodies to do their work on earth and when it's done they leave the body? And if their work is not finished, they come back in a new body? Are we just empty cars waiting for a driver? Are we just disposable suits to be discarded when the Super or Energy Being is finished with us? Perhaps it is a bit of both.

If we look back at history. There are very few people who taught the general population things they need to know in order to live a life that is acceptable to society. Educating the population on everything from the word of God to how to cook food. It is still going on to-day. We are all learning things at different levels. And we are beginning to realise that sometimes we need help and a lot of people turn to prayer. To connect with the Super or Energy Being to extend a helping hand. Jesus was one of them.

Evangelists always ask the new converts to Christianity to ask Christ to enter their body and live his life in them. To become one with them. To help them understand God's design for them. It is a very good indication that indeed Christ was a Super or Energy Being. He was able to walk on water, raise the dead and do other miracles. When the disciples saw him walking towards them on the water, Peter asked Jesus if he can walk on water too. Jesus said yes. But Peter sank after 1 or 2 steps. His faith is not strong enough to hold him up on the water. He has doubts. He needs the Super or Energy Being to hold him up on the water but he does not know how to connect with it and how to use it through faith and prayer.

The world is rapidly changing through technology. Our kids will grow up learning through new technological tools like computers and super-computers, but will they learn what is most important? How to connect with the Energy Being in them. The one who is keeping them going? The one that drives them and gives them new ideas and thoughts? The one who keeps them alive? It is a new way of looking at how we live but perhaps it is something that we should take on consciously. Very often, it is the unconscious that drives us. For example, the heart beats by itself with no control from our conscious mind. Most of our other organs too are controlled by the brain unconsciously. Is it the Super or Energy Being controlling them? If it can perform miracles it must be. Because when it leaves the body, it is lifeless. It cannot move by itself!

If we look at the Universe, or just pictures of a cluster of galaxies and try to imagine how on earth they came into being. We will start to realise that it is indeed an intelligent design by an intelligent Super or Energy Being which is also present in all of us! We should be able to connect with it and the rest of the Universe because it is all seeing, all knowing and all powerful. It can do anything that you ask. All you have to do is connect with it through prayer, affirmations, meditations or whatever you want to call it. It seems that in all cases the Super Being does respond and grant your wishes, whatever you ask for. Then we will start to realise that we are not just empty cars waiting for a driver. The Super or Energy Being is our car and we are the drivers. The only difference is that our Super car can do anything. It can travel to the planets and galaxies. It can heal the sick and raise the dead! We just have to know how to drive it. Our super intelligent, all seeing, all knowing, all powerful car.

I should mention briefly here, that your brain actually programmes our genes through thoughts and words. We actually pass on a lot of our traits to our offspring that way. It is a kind of evolution, in a way, because as we become technologically advanced, our mind also programmes our genes to match or even surpass those advances. It is possible that the Super or Energy Being has a hand in it. Is it why man is progressively becoming smarter? By self-programming with assistance from his Inner Self? I think so. We have power over our destiny in the flesh and in spirit. We can design our future generations by influencing the genes to make the necessary changes with help from the Super Energy Being in all of us. Our thoughts and words is the way to reach them both.

It does make mankind special. The problem is that most people tend to live their lives like empty cars, not knowing who to turn to or what to do most of the time when they run out of options. They just need a few seconds to connect to their Inner Self, Super or Energy Being to rescue them every time. It is not hard to do. Just say "Please help me" a hundred times to your Inner Self in affirmations. Or pray, "Jesus please help me"…and ask whatever you want. You will know that you will be alright if you have faith. Just like walking on water. If you do not believe, your inner self or Super Being or Energy Being will not be able to help you. Why? Because you are telling him, unconsciously, that you do not believe he can do anything for you. In other words you are cancelling your own requests by your own doubts. Don't forget it is all seeing, all knowing and all powerful. It will know your thoughts and what you feel in your heart.

In the next 5,000 million years, before the earth's final demise; when the sun runs out of fuel and grows into a red giant thus consuming and destroying the earth, man will have learned how to become a Super Being by connecting with the Energy Being inside. I have mentioned that man will be able to travel as an Energy Being, who is indestructible, to any part of the Universe. We no longer need the earth, we can settle anywhere we wish in any solar system or galaxy out there. Not in the flesh, which is perishable but as Super Energy Beings that exist forever. Perhaps that is what Christ promised in the New Testament. That we can live forever, if we become one with him? To become a Super Energy Being like him? I think so.

CHAPTER 6. CONCLUSIONS

I believe it is time for us to write the 2nd Testament. The first being the New Testament. It should be a continuation of the Book of Revelations. There has been more miracles in the last 50 years then in the previous 1950 years. We have to write them down for future generations to read about.

When Jesus left he promised to send the Holy Spirit to guide his disciples and mankind. It came to the disciples like a tongue of fire. They were able to perform many miracles in the name of the Lord.

In modern times, everyday people can perform the same miracles, as in the bible. We can change water into wine by adding alcohol and flavours.

We can raise the dead in the hospitals by passing an electric current through their hearts to restart it. We can fly through the air, walk on water, travel under the sea, send messages through the air to be received by radio and televisions thousands of kilometres away.

We can talk to anyone around the world and see them at the other end on a screen. All those things are miracles.

The Holy Spirit has been guiding man for 2,000 years. Are all those modern miracles, revelations from the Holy Spirit? Believers think they are. All those miracles performed by man are revealed to him by the Holy Spirit. The Holy Spirit showed man how to turn water into wine, how to raise the dead, how to walk on water, travel through the air, manufacture medicine and goods and so on.

Without the Holy Spirit man will not be enlightened, he will probably never advance beyond the days of the bible. He would not have become the bright, miracle maker he is today. Do you believe this to be true?

There are many things that man has yet to discover. How can he travel to other parts of the universe? His spaceship is so slow it will take more than 1,000 generations, living in a spaceship, to reach the nearest star at 4 light years away.

Never mind the other billions of stars that are even up to hundreds of light years away.

Every star should have a solar system or planets revolving around it, according to current scientific theory. So every star, in theory, should have living beings in one of its revolving planets. But they are so far away, it is impossible to go there. Unless, we can discover something that only the Holy Spirit or Super Energy Being knows. How to travel at the speed of light or even faster than that. We can get to the nearest star in 4 years instead of 190,000 years. We can travel to anywhere in the universe. The problem is, we do not know how at the moment.

I propose, that if we can recover our galactic memory we may discover that we are actually Energy or Spirit Beings that can travel at the speed of light, unaided in space. We are indestructible. We can take on many forms, human or other.

"Energy cannot be created or destroyed. It can only be changed from one form into another", said scientists. That is what we are. The only way to recover our galactic memory is to become one with the Super Energy Being himself. It is the Super Energy Being that knows where he has been in the last million years. Our flesh and earthly body was only born a few years before and it does not have the power and knowledge of the Super Energy Being.

The Holy Spirit or Super Energy Being will choose when and how to reveal it to us. Maybe sometime in the future when we learn a little bit more about ourselves and the universe we live in and how to become a Super Energy Being.

It seems that man was created and "evolved" through intelligent design. Was it driven by the spirit? The immortal soul? Adam and Eve were punished from the Garden of Eden to live in pain and die forever. God the Son came and gave man God the Holy Spirit to guide and help him. Is that the Energy that drives us all? The Holy Spirit? It has been on Earth for 2,000 years. Since it came, soon after Christ left. It was like
"a tongue of fire" the bible describes it.

It gave the disciples super powers. They were able to perform miracles too, and speak in "tongues". I believe it is the Super Energy Being working through them. They became one with it.

I suggest it is the same thing happening to-day. The evolution of man and ideas, with revelations from the Holy Spirit has helped to develop the world into what it is now. Man can recreate all the miracles in the bible and more. Man can even predict what is going to happen 5 billion years from now. The end of the earth, when the sun runs out of its fuel. Man has learned to become a miracle maker but has yet to become a Super Energy Being. If you were to travel back to the days of the bible and show them what you have to-day, they will probably worship you as a God. We have evolved into highly sophisticated beings with many technological advancements but not yet Super Beings.

According to current scientific theory, the sun is 5,000 million years old. It is half way through its life cycle. In another 5,000 million years it will expand into a red giant 100 million times bigger than its normal size. It will become so hot on earth that we can only conclude it will be burned. The sea will boil. Then the sun will collapse into a white dwarf or a black hole.

Man will have to move off somewhere. If earth is not destroyed by pollution first. I propose that man will leave as a Spirit or Energy Being and populate other solar systems and beyond. The miracles man creates everyday are revelations from the ultimate power that drives him and the Universe, God the Holy Spirit. The Holy Spirit. The Immortal Soul. The Energy Being. We were created in his image. Us the Super Energy Beings in the making. We just don't know it yet.

Finally, I want to comment on the relationship between ancient and biblical knowledge and scientific explanations regarding god, evolution and man's destiny.

There are many religions and beliefs on earth, but they all seem to promote one thing and that is the "inner self, the spirit, the mind, enlightenment, everlasting life and god". There are many other references but they are all included in those six concepts.

It will take many books to discuss those six concepts, and many other authors have written about them, but I would like to comment on something that no one else has pointed out before. That is the relationship between your thoughts, your spoken words and your genetic being or makeup.

Have you ever wondered why your children sometimes behave and do things like you? Or your parents? We often say that our child has taken after grandpa, because he/she sometimes speak or behave like grandpa. How does that come about? I propose that when you think or speak, it is recorded by your brain like a computer records all information typed into it. That is why you remember what you said or thought about yesterday or even years before. It is recorded in your brain and **also your genetic makeup.** It is passed on to your children and descendants. Sometimes those traits are expressed sometimes they are not, in genetic terms.

I would like to expand on it a bit more. When you speak, meditate or pray you are writing those information onto your genetic makeup. If you keep on repeating that message, it will be magnified by the brain and expressed immediately as in affirmations. Salesmen use affirmations to achieve something they want by repeating that goal a thousand times a day or so.

They repeat it so many times that in a few days they believe in it with so much conviction that the customer too can feel the power of his words. His belief in his product convinced the customer to buy the product because the belief has been transferred to them through his presentation.

The same thing works with prayer. When Christians pray they are convinced by the power of their words, which is also transferred to their listeners. Non-believers can hear and feel the power of their words and convert to Christianity. The prayers are sometimes repeated so many times, like the Lord's prayer, that it actually creates the change through magnification and genetic effect. How did the ancients know about this? Through trial and error? Through divine intervention? As in the stories of the bible? It is said in the bible in the old testament that God… "effects his revenge on man down to the 3rd or 4th generation". Is it because the spoken "word of God is magnified and passed on in the genes to later generations"?.

Re-incarnation works in the same way. The objective is to strive for enlightenment and purity of the heart or soul. Through meditation or prayer the genetic effect takes place by magnification in the brain and subsequent recording in the genes. Practitioners of reincarnation believe that when you achieve a certain level of enlightenment and purity you return to earth as a higher being, in the next life cycle.

We can extrapolate my proposal to include all things to do with the spoken words, thoughts and their genetic expression. Sorcery, witchcraft, black magic and so on. They all work in the same way with Christian prayers, meditation or affirmations. How did the ancient practitioners of sorcery, black magic and so on knew? Through the power of the spoken words, its magnification by the brain and their recording and expression by the genes. Genes are all powerful because they control what you become. Your height, colour, number of teeth, eyes, nails, everything. Even how your brain works!

It is amazing! Isn't it? Now we can see or glimpse how it works. But who is in control of it all? Does our brain and genes work independently to turn us this way or that way? To make you feel good to-day and bad tomorrow? Evolutionary theory proposed by many Scientists to date suggest that it is selection or survival of the fittest that controls it. That only the good traits survive and the bad ones die off. But I venture to say, it is you and your spoken words that control it. Whether it is expressed through your genes depends on whether your brain magnifies it enough to be recorded. It is similar to one person versus a 1000 working on the same thing. You'll notice the effect quickly when there are 1000 people behind it versus one person.

But who controls you? That is my point. It is the Spirit Being, the Super Energy Being, God that controls you. Or controls the whole universe. We are still human made of bone, flesh and blood. Made by super beings much more intelligent than we are. We are being trained to be super beings ourselves. Our technology now will make us Gods in the eyes of St Peter and the apostles and the people of their day. In 1,000 million years who knows what we can do?

I propose that we should speed it up by programming ourselves through the spoken word, whether you pray, meditate or use other techniques. Magnify our good qualities so we can record them in our genes and pass them on to our descendants. Then we can become Super Energy Beings much quicker, perhaps like God himself.

I feel that I have touched on and explained every point that need to be explored to show that God is indeed energy itself. God is all seeing and all powerful. God is the Super Energy Being in all of us. The only way to be one with it is to ask him to be one with you and live through you. Then you will notice the power that comes through your spoken words. Then you will access your "galactic memory" and know where you have been in the last million years or since the beginning of the Universe.

Whether you choose to become one with God or not is up to you. But just like the rain and the sunshine, you too will also become a super being in the future. God will not deny you life giving rain or sunshine just because you don't believe or have lost your way. Do you Believe?

About the author…

Semisi Pone is a graduate of the University of Auckland. He graduated in 1985 with a BSc and a MSc (Hons) in 1989. He has worked overseas in Tonga as a Plant Pathologist and Senior Plant Virologist, the University of the South Pacific in Samoa as a Fellow, the South Pacific Commission in Fiji as an Advisor and Head of the Plant Protection Services and also did some work for the United Nations (FAO, Rome) in one of its expert panels and Regional Plant Protection Organisation technical meetings.

He has also worked in various places and jobs in Auckland. He is interested in the topic of "man's mortality" and the "immortal soul" hence this book. He believes that it is something "worth discussing around the dinner table".

He also writes books in other genre mainly humour, poetry, fiction, non-fiction, stories for kids and anything else that he is interested in. He has retired from Science and considers himself a "full-time writer".

Semisi Pone has published more that 60 books and ebooks in New Zealand and on the internet. You can see these books in Blurb.com, Apple i-bookstores, Amazon Kindle and Amazon Create Space bookstores.

www.ingramcontent.com/pod-product-compliance
Lightning Source LLC
Chambersburg PA
CBHW061302040426
42444CB00010B/2487